C000257680

SOUTHERN COLOUR TO THE WEST
Dorset, Somerset, Devon and Cornwall

Compiled by Kevin Robertson

© Kevin Robertson (Noodle Books) 2010

ISBN   978-1-906419-38-7

First published in 2010 by Kevin Robertson
under the **NOODLE BOOKS** imprint
PO Box 279
Corhampton
SOUTHAMPTON
SO32 3ZX

www.noodlebooks.co.uk

Printed in England by The Information Press

Front cover - An Exeter to Padstow service on the unmistakable Meldon Viaduct. In charge is a BR 'Standard Tank' attached to what is perhaps slightly unusually, two brake composites.

David Smith

Frontispiece - One of the big, Urie (rebuilt from Drummond) 'H15' class 4-6-0 class, No. 30489 seen heading west near Amesbury Junction with milk tanks for the West Country. Built in 1914, this engine was for some time based at Nine Elms but later moved to Eastleigh. In a 47 year life, it ran just over 1.5 million miles. 17 August 1959.

Bottom - An unidentified 'Pacific' having just passed Pottington Signal Box and swing bridge on the outskirts of Barnstaple with a train from Ilfracombe.

David Smith

Back cover - Busy times at Exeter Central - see also page 48.

David Smith

Note - unaccredited views and those shown as Peter Elliott and Roger Thornton are in the KR / Noodle Books collection. Where known, dates are shown.

Contents

INTRODUCTION

There has always been something slightly romantic in the thought of a trip from Waterloo - west to Devon and into Cornwall. Destinations such as Ilfracombe, Padstow, Bude all so different to the suburbs of the metropolis.

The Southern Railway and later the Southern Region were very clever in their marketing, names such as the 'Atlantic Coast Express' and 'Devon Belle' guaranteed to stir the imagination.

So far as the operators were concerned, it was later that commercialism began to take over from romanticism when it came to the practicalities of running a service. The nationalised network was seen as a drain on resources a government said the country did not possess. Sacrifices would have to be made to the minority to preserve the majority. The result, as we know, was the Beeching report. Whilst to the enthusiast the very mention of that name is almost guaranteed to raise the temperature, it must be realised that if it had not been him, then someone else would have behaved in an identical fashion.

Half a century ago it could not have been foreseen that the railways might enjoy a revival, although whether that revival is truly what present day politicians will have us believe or a response to an ever congested road system, is a matter for debate.

Whatever, the chance of a revival of railways to most of the former Southern routes in the West Country is unlikely. The exception being the main line from Okehampton through Tavistock to Bere Alston and eventually Plymouth.

For the remainder trains will only exist in photographs - albums such as this. So put aside the present and venture back into the past. To the un-pruned Southern network in Dorset, Somerset, Devon and Cornwall.

(Intentionally, the captions have been kept deliberately brief, the reader is likely to know the locations themselves, even if not personally, certainly from photographs. There is also more space for the actual views!)

In concluding this brief narrative, I would like to thank those whose work or collections have been used: Peter Elliott, Les Elsey, Paul Hersey, Bruce Murray, the John Knottley collection - courtesy of The Swanage Railway Trust, David Smith, Roger Thornton and Tony Woodforth.

Kevin Robertson

Opposite, top - The 'Atlantic Coast Express', for many years the prestige train of the West of England line and somewhat longer lived than the 'Devon Belle' which ran only from 1947 to 1954. Waiting to leave Waterloo on the start of the journey is 'Merchant Navy' No. 35018 *'British India Line'*, which will work through to Exeter shedding coaches at Salisbury for the various branches west to Exeter. At Exeter the train will again divide, going forward as separate portions to Plymouth and Ilfracombe - with sub division again for Bude and Padstow. **Opposite, bottom -** Down milk empties near Pirbright behind a 'Merchant Navy', possibly No. 35007 *'Aberdeen Commonwealth'*. **Top -** A slippery start for No. 34064 *'Fighter Command'* leaving Andover.
Bottom - For a while the members of the 'Schools' class based at Nine Elms, found employment on Waterloo - Salisbury semi-fast turns, occasionally venturing as far as Yeovil. No. 30913 *'Christ's Hospital'* is viewed leaving Andover for Salisbury.

Les Elsey - 1 and The John Knottley collection, courtesy of The Swanage Railway Trust–1

Variations in motive power at Salisbury

Opposite top - Another 'Schools', this time No. 30910 *'Merchant Taylors'* in somewhat grimy condition with what appears to be Nine Elms duty No. 22. For a time this working was the province of a BR 'Standard Class 5', although regardless of the locomotive, the turn began with the engine leaving Nine Elms at 4.03 am ready for the 4.45 am to Yeovil Junction. The loco would then go to Yeovil Town for turning, returning with the 2.45 pm from Yeovil arriving at Salisbury at 4.27 pm: which is probably the point at which it was photographed. After shunting the West sidings, departure was at 5.15 pm and a final return to Nine Elms at 9.14 pm. Four sets of men were involved.

Opposite bottom - An engine that survives in preservation today, No. 34007 *'Wadebridge'* arranged together with several items of typical Southern paraphernalia: the lamp, station sign, loud speakers and seat. Built in 1945, 34007 (originally 21C107) the engine survived just 20 years in service, before being sold for scrap and subsequently languishing for almost 16 years at the infamous Barry scrapyard. It was rescued in 1981 and following restoration returned to steam in 2006.   Peter Elliott

Above - The other prestige train on the West of England line was the 'Atlantic Coast Express', the name selected following a competition amongst the staff in the July 1925 'Southern Railway Magazine'. Departure from Waterloo was at 11.00 am, the service stopping at Salisbury where it split, the front portion for Exeter and beyond with the rear portion serving the principal intermediate stations and branch liens en-route. At Exeter the train again split, with sections for Plymouth - the latter splitting again at Okehampton with separate portions for Padstow and Bude, and Ilfracombe. In all then a cosmopolitan train but one where the guard had also to ensure passengers were in the correct portion. Such was the popularity of the service that it was not unknown for several relief trains to operate. In the reverse direction things were slightly easier, the main train assembled at Exeter and then running to Waterloo with just one intermediate stop at Salisbury. It is upon leaving Salisbury, with the 'up' working that we see 'Merchant Navy' No. 35022 *'Holland America Line'* departing on the last leg of the journey, often run to a mile–a–minute schedule.

Above - 'Battle of Britain', No. 34058 *'Sir Frederick Pile'* passing through the Southern station at Wilton. It was here that the 'Devon Belle' would stop to change engines, so making the latter train the only regular passenger working not to call at Salisbury. **Bottom** - Stopping passenger, west of Salisbury, No. '30798 *'Sir Hectimere'* in its last years of service. The engine had moved to Salisbury in June 1959 and remained in use until June 1962 at which time it was 32 years old and had completed just over one million miles.

Opposite top - Even less of a train for standard 'Class 3' No. 82030 hauling two Bulleid coaches near, it is believed, Crewkerne.   David Smith

Opposite bottom - The use of Bulleid Pacifics on freight was always more common the West of England line compared with the Bournemouth route. No. 34099 *'Lynmouth'* performing the role sometime between February 1960 and September 1961.   David Smith

Above - Busy days at Yeovil Town with BR Standard, SR and GWR designs present. An average of 20 loco-motives were allocated here although engines from other depots would also arrive for servicing between duties - No. 34059 probably fitting this criteria. Unusually the shed did not have a turntable, although one was provided at the nearby Yeovil Junction Station.

Bottom - Operating between Yeovil Town and Yeovil Junction was a regular shuttle service, the 1¾ mile journey timetabled to take an average of five minutes start to stop. In charge on this occasion was 'M7. No. 30131. On the left is the line to the WR at Yeovil Pen Mill.

The John Knottley collection, courtesy of The Swanage Railway Trust

Axminster and the Lyme Regis Branch

From 1903 until 1965 it was possible to travel by train from Axminster in Devon to the Dorset coast at Lyme Regis. Due to its light construction, initially two former LBSCR 'Terrier' tanks were acquired by the LSWR to work the line, LSWR Nos. 734 and 735, although at this early stage the actual route was in the ownership of an independent company.

As was often the case with privately funded branch lines, the initial euphoria expressed by the owners did not translate into a viable business and the undertaking was sold to the LSWR from 1907.

In the days prior to the motor car traffic was reasonable, excursion traffic another useful source of revenue. Following the departure of the 'Terrier' tanks, for most of its life the seven mile line was worked almost exclusively by Adams 4-4-2 'Radial' tank engines. These increasingly antiquated machines the subject of much interest and indeed visits from enthusiasts - although it was ironic that many of those same enthusiasts probably reached Axminster by car! Over the years varying types of locomotive were tried as replacements for the ageing LSWR engines, including in 1930 an 'LBSCR' D1 and in BR days a former GWR 'Pannier Tank', neither was successful.

The normal branch train would consist of one or two coaches, supplemented on summer weekends with through coaches off the 'Atlantic Coast Express'. This could increase the load to perhaps as many as six vehicles and meaning double heading with two 'Radials' was required.

Eventually age took its inevitable toll and in 1961 BR Standard 'Class 2' tank engines took over from the LSWR machines. In the very last months a single unit diesel railcars was used.

Bottom - No. 30583 waiting at the end of the bay at Axminster station seemingly with the coal supply in the bunker being attended to. Water for Combpyne would often be carried in cans on the front framing of the engine.

Axminster and the Lyme Regis Branch - pages 12 –17

This page: Axminster and Combpyne, pages 14 and 15: Lyme Regis.

The home depot for the engines working the branch was Exmouth Junction, BR code, 72A although up to 1962 the small shed at the terminus was also used for basic servicing requirements - the corner of the latter can just be seen above the bunker of the engine on this page. 'Pull-Push' working was not employed on the line and consequently there was a requirement for the engine to run-round at either end of the 20 minute journey.

Pages 12 & 13 are three views of 'Radial' and BR Standard 'Class 2' tank engines against the buffers and at Combpyne .At the latter point, the line commenced to curve west, it then continued on this westerly course until just after Hook Farm, before swinging almost due south again to the terminus. Prior to 1930, Combpyne had boasted a run-round loop and signal box, but economy dictated these be removed so effecting a saving in both maintenance and staffing costs. Goods traffic was a feature here from what was an agricultural area whilst the Camping Coach in the background was a regular feature for many years.

Pages 14 / 15 - No. 30584 receiving attention at Lyme Regis prior to returning to Axminster and a view of the engine shed in the background. 'You have not recorded perhaps by best side', remarked the driver to the photographer after taking the view.

Pages 16 & 17 overleaf - Variations in motive power at Lyme Regis. Nos. 30583 and 30584 plus one of their BR steam replacements, No. 41206. Also seen is a single WR 'Bubble-car' unit that took over for the last months of operation. Freight has clearly already ceased.

David Smith - 5, Peter Elliott - 2

Seaton Junction and the Seaton Branch

The 4¼ mile branch from the junction with the main line at Seaton Junction to the coastal terminus at Seaton dated from 1868 with the Junction station rebuilt by the Southern Railway with typical angular concrete in 1937. With a population in 1900 of just 1,300 soles at Seaton, the little railway was never likely to generate much traffic by itself, the same applying to the two intermediate stopping places of Colyford and Colyton. Even so on summer Saturdays, traffic was brisk with up to 500 trippers arriving from Waterloo, often in through coaches. Such peaks though were not what the 1960s railway wanted, and with the SR having been forced to pass the route to the Western Region in 1962, closure came in March 1966. Part of the trackbed is now used for an electric tramway, running from Seaton as far as Colyford, just one mile from the original Junction station.

Peter Elliott and Roger Thornton

Sidmouth Junction and the Sidmouth Branch

The branch lines to Sidmouth and Exmouth, the latter via Budleigh Salterton, diverged from the main LSWR West of England line at the appropriately named Sidmouth Junction, splitting again immediately south of Tipton St Johns with one line continuing to Sidmouth and the other meandering through the delightfully named Newton Poppleford, East Budleigh, Budleigh Salterton and Littleham to reach Exmouth.

This was another relatively early branch line, opened in 1874, but with the station at Sidmouth located in typical railway fashion a mile from the town centre.

Seen above, 'M7' No. 30024 leaves the Exmouth branch in its wake as its head off towards Sidmouth - an Exmouth line train is also just visible in the background.

Tipton St Johns has already been referred to, but what has not been mentioned is that this rural location was at one time witness to no less than 50 train movements per day - now there are none. Perhaps because of its more well to do and fashionable location - Sidmouth had a theatre as early as 1905 - the railway to the town survived as an independent company until as late as 1923, despite the fact it had done everything in its power to discourage 'day-trippers' up to this time.

Up to 1903, the railway from the main line junction ventured only to Sidmouth, but it was in this year that the eastwards route to Exmouth was inaugurated. As such it was possible to instigate a round, Exeter - Exmouth (via Topsham) - Sidmouth Junction - Exeter service, even if a reversal was required at Exmouth.

Neither the Sidmouth branch nor the line through Budleigh Salterton would survive the Beeching axe, both were closed to passengers in March 1967.

Exmouth Junction and Exmouth Branch

The original branch line to Exmouth diverged at the junction of the same name.

Again built by an independent company - who had been persuaded to give up their original broad-gauge ambitions - the line was opened in 1861 and absorbed into the LSWR just five years later.

Unlike the branches to Lyme Regis, Seaton and Sidmouth, Exmouth was, even it its earliest days, a commuter town for Exeter. Traffic thus built steadily, so much so that by 1914 the original single line from Exmouth Junction as far as the first station at Topsham had been doubled.

Regular traffic also demanded no less than 31 services between Exeter and Exmouth in 1957, supplemented by a 'short' train operating just between Exeter and Topsham.

En-route there were intermediate goods facilities to Topsham Quay and Exmouth Docks and whilst the line survives today, both the aforementioned freight facilities were closed many years ago.

In the view below, Ivatt 2-6-2T No. 41318 has charge of a branch service, south of Topsham.

As with the other branches mentioned, this line had also been proposed for closure but fortunately sense prevailed and it still enjoys a lively commuter service.

Opposite page - Servicing steam locomotives for Exmouth branch trains, as well as the many main line workings, was at the big Exeter depot of Exmouth Junction/. This was sited opposite to the point of divergence of the branch. At the west end of the site was the location of the Southern concrete works.

David Smith (right)

The Bournemouth area

Bournemouth fits conveniently into the Dorset area with lines arriving from the east, north west, north east and west. In the view above, a grimy rebuilt 'West Country' No. 34045 *'Combe Martin'* is running on the 'old road' from Wimborne, just north of Bournemouth, with what may well be a through working diverted on to this line.

Opposite top - Introduced in 1951, 'The Royal Wessex' was one of five 'Festival' trains named by British Railways during the year. In many ways also it was a logical successor to the pre-war 'Bournemouth Limited'. The 1951 service afforded a through working between Waterloo and Weymouth once each way daily, as well as coaches to separate coaches to serve Bournemouth West and Swanage. In the view seen, 'Merchant Navy' No. 35008 *'Orient Line'* has charge of the train.

Opposite bottom - Another exceedingly grimy engine. Masquerading under all that dirt is a BR Standard 'Class 5', believed to be No. 73001, seen climbing Parkstone bank on what was clearly a warm summers day. The train has come off the Somerset and Dorset line - see also pages 31 to 35 - as witness the maroon coaching stock. The front vehicle of which is to GWR Hawkesworth design.

David Smith - 3

Bournemouth and Branksome

In the Bournemouth area, locomotive facilities were provided at Bournemouth Central and Branksome, the latter used by locomotives working trains to and from the Somerset & Dorset line. The depot at Branksome would also act as a servicing point for engines on main line workings having a short-turnaround.

Top left - Standing on the spur at the end of the turntable at Bournemouth central loco is Standard 'Class 4' 76008. A number of these locomotives arrived on the region in the 1950s, in so doing consigning many former LSWR 4-4-0 types to scrap. The rust streaks on the rear of the tender are the effect of chemical added to soften the hard water of the area.

Bottom left - Awaiting to back down to Bournemouth West, 'Merchant Navy' No. 35024 *East Asiatic Company* stands in Branksome shed yard. (The east curve is in the background.) Entering service in November 1948, the engine was rebuilt in the form seen here 11 years later and withdrawn in January 1965 having run 839, 415 recorded miles.

Above - With a slightly perplexing 'Wareham - Swanage' headcode, 'Lord Nelson' No. 30850 rounds the curve off Gas Works Viaduct heading fro Bournemouth West. This is likely to be an empty stock working.

David Smith - 2

Pages 26 and 27 overleaf - Left-hand page: Branksome triangle to and from Bournemouth West.
Right-hand page: Trains on the 1-60 of Parkstone bank. In the top view the service may very well be a working from Swanage.

David Smith

Above - In green livery - just, 'Battle of Britain' No. 34056 *'Croydon'* waits at Poole. The white painted hinges on the smokebox door may indicate recent railtour duty.

David Smith

Bottom - With the fireman careful watching the injector, BR Standard 'Class 5' No. 73155 leaves Dorchester South for Bournemouth in charge of a eight coach train of what appears to be mainly Bulleid stock but with a BR built Restaurant Car. The signal box seen here was a 1959 replacement for the original 1878 structure.

Roger Thornton

Above - Arriving at Broadstone with a train from Ringwood and Wimborne is 'M7' No. 30060. In the background are the home signals allowing services from Corfe Mullen on the Somerset & Dorset line.

Bottom - Special working at Hamworthy. 7 June 1958. The tour was organised by the 'Railway Enthusiasts Club' and took in Poole, Hamworthy, Melcombe Regis, Portland, Easton, Maiden Newton and Bournemouth West. The smokebox plate of the 'M7' No. 30107, has a distinctly Scottish colour scheme.

David Smith and Roger Thornton

Somerset & Dorset Workings

Services on and off the S &D would invariably bring LMS locomotives to Bournemouth which were serviced at Branksome.

Left - Templecombe based LMS '2P' No. 40583, was recorded at Branksome shed on the same occasion as 35024 - seen on page 24. Notice the automatic tablet catcher just visible on the tender of No. 40583.

Above - Bournemouth West with S & D 2-8-0 and Southern 'Mogul' side by side. The pigeon baskets are a reminder of a regular traffic once handled by the railways in the south, the S & D in particular.

Bottom - Nos. 40697 and 34042 *'Dorchester'* burst out of the gloom of Windsor Hill Tunnel with a Bournemouth West to Manchester working. 22 July 1961.   David Smith - 2, Tony Molyneaux - 1

Pages 32 / 33 overleaf - Nos. 75027 and 34029 near Chilcompton.   Tony Molyneaux

The Somerset & Dorset at Radstock and Corfe Mullen

Left - Leaving Radstock on the down line towards Midsomer Norton. A BR Standard 'Class 4' is about to pass over the level crossing immediately south of the station. **This page -** Corfe Mullen. It was here that the original Dorset Central Railway turned east to joint the LSWR at Wimborne, meaning trains for Bournemouth were faced with a reversal at the former location. This situation lasted until 1884/5 when a three mile single line connection was built direct to Broadstone, following which the Wimborne connection was relegated to only occasional use and became a truncated siding in 1933. In the top view No. 76015 is northbound with a local working, the erstwhile Wimborne connection diverging to the left. In the bottom view, Ivatt 'Class 2' No. 41283 catches the evening sun as it heads north past Corfe Mullen signal box on the double line to Bailey Gate.   David Smith

Wareham and Swanage Branch

Pages 36 / 37 - Wareham, main line. With the bay used by Swanage branch trains on the left, a rebuilt 'Battle of Britain' Pacific leaves the station westbound for Dorchester and Weymouth.   Peter Elliott

Opposite top - On what is a local working between Bournemouth Central and Weymouth, BR Standard 'Class 4' 2-6-4T No. 80017 deposits seemingly even more waiting passengers on to the platform at Wareham.

Opposite bottom - 'M7' No. 30108 crossing typical Dorset heath land on the Swanage branch.

This page, top - The unmistakable location of the viaduct just north of Corfe Castle station.

This page, bottom - Passing evidence of the narrow gauge mineral railways north of Corfe Castle, 'M7' No. 30057 has charge of the branch working, plus what appears to be a through coach at the end of the train.

                    The John Knottley collection, courtesy of The Swanage Railway Trust - 1, David Smith - 3

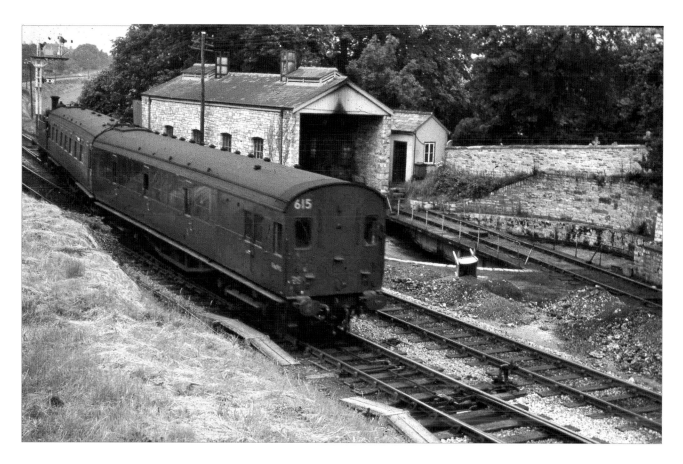

Swanage and the Main Line

Branch services to Swanage usually consisted of a shuttle working from Wareham, calling at the one intermediate stopping place of Corfe Castle. Apart from the usual passenger facilities at Swanage - there was also an extensive goods yard and goods shed, locomotive servicing facilities and a turntable were provided. The latter to cope with engines arriving with excursion trains. Most of the buildings were also built from local Purbeck stone. **Opposite page** - 'Pull-Push' and non 'Pull-Push' trains with an unidentified 'M7' and 'BR Standard 'Class 4' 2-6-4T No. 80032, the latter on a conventional loco hauled working. **This page top** - Summer traffic, by both road and rail at Swanage. 'M7' No. 30667 waits in the bay platform whilst in the background is main line stock from a through train, stabled and awaiting time for the return. The road coaches are similarly parked until the time comes for their own return trips. **Bottom** - 'N' class 2-6-0 No. 31853 on a Bournemouth West to Dorchester working.

Paul Hersey - 1, Roger Thornton - 1, Peter Elliott - 1, David Smith

West to Exeter

Pages 42 / 43, and left - leaving (and approaching) Exeter Central with Nos. 35007 '*Aberdeen Common-wealth*' and 34023 '*Blackmore Vale*'. In the view opposite top, St James' Park Halt may be seen in the background. **This page** - Nos. 34059 (top) and 35003 (bottom) shortly after departure. In the top view, the vehicle behind the tender had distinct similarities to a GWR auto-coach. David Smith - 5

Exeter Central

Conveniently located in the centre of the City, 'Central' or as it was formerly known 'Queen Street', was, during steam days, a busy interchange point, as well as the limit of westward operation for the big 'Merchant Class' type. Hence there was the need for numerous engine changes. The plethora of 'Light Pacifics' operated by the Southern Region also meant such engines might be seen on lesser workings: No. 34005 *'Barnstaple'* recorded twice with the same working but at slightly different locations. Also seen is a Standard 'Class 4' and a Standard 'Class 3' 2-6-2T No. 82010, the latter departing on an Exeter - Exmouth working.   David Smith - 4

Exeter Central

The present day design of Exeter Central dates from 1933, although much track rationalisation has taken place from the mid 1960s onwards. Prior to that time up to 73 bogie coaches could be stabled, split between the sidings at the west and east ends of the station, some at the latter end under covered accommodation. With the regular splitting and make up of main line trains, there was a corresponding large number of light engine movements.

Top left - 'Merchant Navy' No. 35029 and an unidentified unrebuilt 'Light Pacific' stand awaiting movement, the former destined for Exmouth Junction. Notice how on No. 35029 the cleaning gangs have been unable to reach the top of the boiler.

Bottom - To the left No. 34086 *'219 Squadron'* waits for its own eastbound working as No. 35008 *'Orient Line'* arrives from Waterloo.

Opposite top - No. 34086 now with its own train departs east past the former 'A' signal box.

Opposite bottom - A lightweight load of a 3-coach BR Mk1 set in green plus 4-wheel van for No. 34072 *'257 Squadron'*.

David Smith

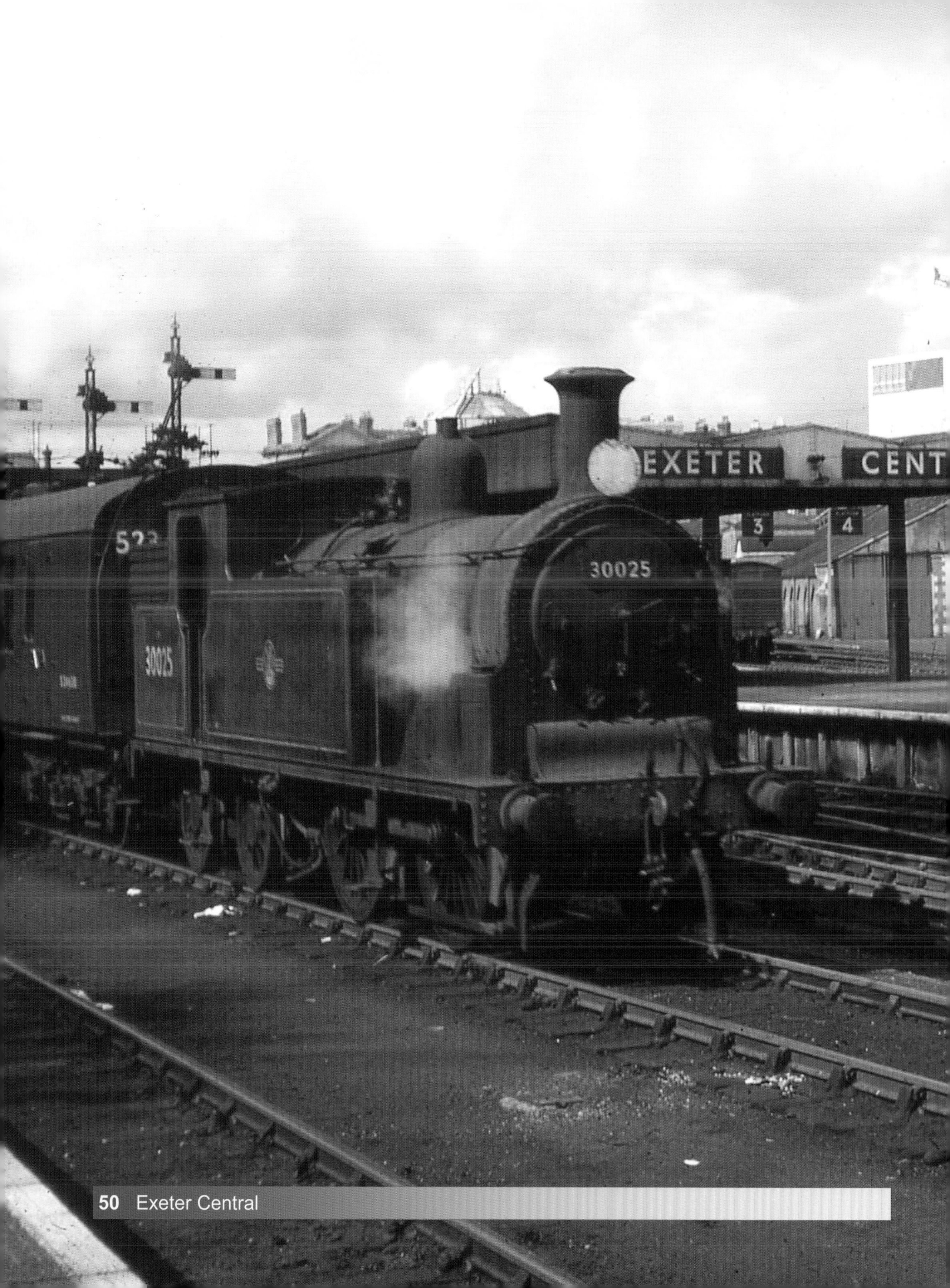

50 Exeter Central

Exeter Central

This page top, and pages 50 / 51 - station pilot duties for 'M7' No 30025.

Bottom - Front end assistance for an 'S15' class 4-6-0 up the 1 in 37 bank from St Davids in the form of 'W' class 2-6-4T No. 31911. The latter were replacements for the 'Z' class tank engines. No doubt further pushing power was provided at the rear of the train.

Opposite top - No. 34086 *'219 Squadron'* again, this time facing west, recently arrived from Exmouth Junction depot with the tender full and ready for duty via Crediton.

Opposite bottom and pages 54 / 55 - No. 34036 *'Westward Ho!'* displaying wooden cabside window surrounds (on some members of the class they were painted green) and seemingly with steam to spare.

The John Knottley collection, courtesy of The Swanage Railway Trust – 6

The Western Route

To maintain driver familiarity, there were regular turns for Southern men with SR locomotives over the Western Region route via Dawlish: similarly for Western men with their engines via Okehampton. This was so that in case of emergency each would be familiar with the other's line.

Right - No. 34060 *'25 Squadron'* is alongside the famous Dawlish sea-wall. **Bottom** - No. 34002 *'Salisbury'*, light engine at Newton Abbot.

The John Knottley collection, courtesy of The Swanage Railway Trust - 1

Opposite page - Cowley Bridge Junction

North of Exeter St Davids, was the point of divergence for Southern lines into west Devon and Cornwall. For years a bottleneck, Cowley Bridge was also a place where the signalman would be involved in true regulation of trains - especially if a service were running late. In the top view 'N' class No. 31860 comes off the SR route onto the western with mixed freight. In the lower view, it is the turn of 'West Country' 34032 *'Camelford'*. Notwithstanding the pruning of the SR route, the junction is still required today, albeit consisting a single lead to a single set of rails to Barnstaple and Okehampton.

David Smith - 2

West of Exeter - trains in the landscape, pages 58 to 60.
Opposite top - No. 34072 *'257 Squadron'* with what is believed to be an Exeter - Ilfracombe working.
Opposite bottom - A Padstow line service finds 'T9' No. 30715 in charge of a mixed passenger and freight working.
Above - On the route from Exeter to Plymouth, 'N' class No. 31830.
Bottom - West Country, at an unreported location, but probably on the Torrington branch. The bunker end of the 'Ivatt' tank devoid of the requisite brackets to take the normal line route code. **Page 60**, top - 34002 *'Salisbury'* on the Southern Plymouth main line. **Page 60,** bottom - The 'Exmoor Ranger' railtour of 27 March 1965. David Smith - 4, Roger Thornton - 1

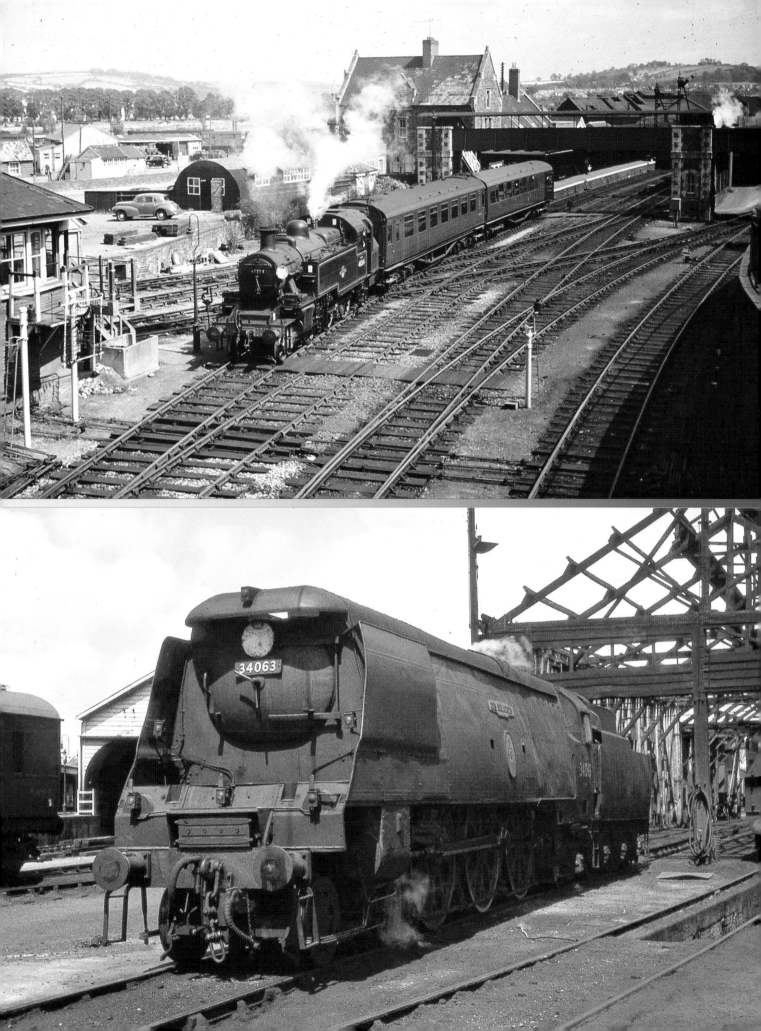

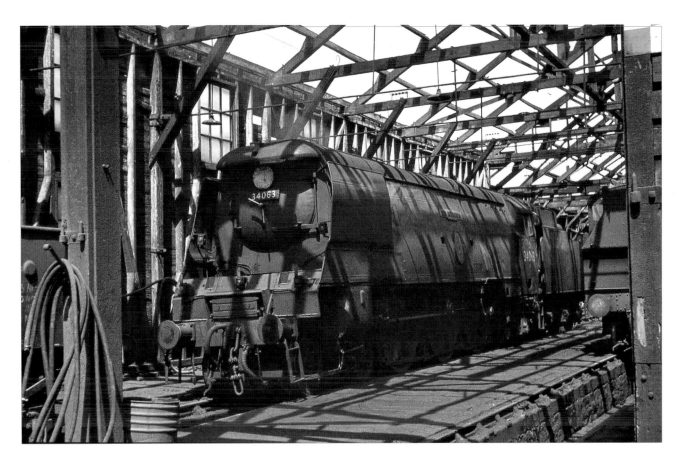

Barnstaple Junction

One of what were once three stations at Barnstaple, the former Junction location nowadays the only one to survive, albeit as little more than a stub siding. In more affluent days, the station was in effect a cross-roads, for the routes to and from Exeter, Ilfracombe, Torrington and Taunton: the latter a former GW line arriving at Barnstaple Victoria Road. Further back in time, Barnstaple Town had itself been the junction for the narrow gauge line to Lynton. This much lamented railway is nowadays in the process of slowly being returned to use. Following transfer of the Southern lines west of Salisbury to the Western Region, a number of former SR steam engines came under the control of the WR, resulting in various transfers between the regions. Then as lines were closed and steam operation declined generally, the WR were responsible for the withdrawal of some Bulleid Pacifics although other engines, including No. 41312, seen on page 61, was transferred back to the Southern and ended its days at Eastleigh.

Page 61, top - Ivatt 'Class 2', No. 41312 takes the Bideford / Torrington route at the Junction, 31 July 1962. The Ilfracombe route diverges to the opposite side of the signal box.

Page 61, bottom - AWS fitted 'Battle of Britain' No. 34063 *'229 Squadron'* outside the remains of the roofless, yet still operational steam shed at Barnstaple Junction. The goods shed building is just visible on the extreme left.

Opposite, top - From Barnstaple, locomotives were supplied to the sub-sheds at Torrington and Ilfracombe, no pacifics ever allocated to Barnstaple. No. 34063 was an Exmouth Junction engine, no doubt stabled here between duties.

Opposite bottom - Several 'N' class 2-6-0s were allocated here, although No. 31834 was again a visitor from Exmouth Junction. Both the engines referred to display an Ilfracombe line headcode disc.

This page - Trains for Exeter awaiting departure: inset No. 34079 is seen.

The John Knottley collection, courtesy of The Swanage Railway Trust - 3, Tony Woodforth collection - 1, Peter Elliott - 1

The Ilfracombe Line

Top - Braunton Station, seen north towards Ilfracombe.

Bottom left - No. 34081 *'92 Squadron'* with a 10-coach load on the Ilfracombe line.

Bottom right - Western Region influence in colour schemes.

Opposite top - No. 34072 *'257 Squadron'* climbing the bank near Heddon Mill level crossing bound for Ilfracombe.

Opposite bottom - Double heading on the departure from Ilfracombe and climbing the 1 in 36 bank.

David Smith - 2, Tony Woodforth collection - 2

Ilfracombe

The station here was some 254 feet above sea level, hence the degree of protection from the elements for the platform. Double heading was also commonplace, the gradient obvious from the photographs. **Pages 66 / 67** - Conversation time before departure: notice the hand-lamp. **Top** - Private cars and taxies, from here there was once a railway operated bus service six miles to Combe Martin. **Bottom -** The windbreak added to the westwards facing side of the platform in 1892. **Opposite top** - No. 34070 *'Manston'* awaiting departure. **Opposite bottom -** The carriage sidings. Additional facilities including, new sidings, run-round loop, and general station improvements were undertaken by the Southern from 1924 onwards. Tony Woodforth collection - 4, Peter Elliott - 2

Ilfracombe

The locomotive facilities at Ilfracombe were simple but sufficient. A shed with inspection pit, shed avoiding line and turntable, the latter, unlike that at Barnstaple Junction, able to accommodate the 'West Country'/ 'Battle of Britain' type pacifics. Even as the line passed the shed area it was already climbing, the whole station site then at the foot of a steep gradient: hence the prohibition of shunting coaching by gravity alone.

In the right hand view an unidentified .Mogul' is alongside the shed whilst below, a 'Pacific' is in the same position.

It is believed the absolute peak so far as summer traffic was concerned occurred in the 1958 season, after which followed a rapid decline. Full closure came just 12 years later in 1970, although by that time, much of the infrastructure had already been removed, with the last services operated by a shuttle DMU service.

Peter Elliott and Tony Molyneaux

The Torrington Branch

The railway originally reached Torrington from the direction of Barnstaple via Bideford in 1872. Nine years later it ceased to be a true terminus with the construction of the Torrington & Marland mineral line, although this was to the 3 foot gauge.

Early in the 20th century, powers were obtained to extend from Torrington to Halwill, utilising for part of the route the course of the former mineral line. This was finally achieved in 1925, although by comparison with the easily graded route from Barnstaple, the extension was very much switchback in nature with a gradient as steep as 1 in 40 in places.

At Torrington, apart from passengers and general freight, there was regular milk traffic and whilst passenger services ceased in 1965, milk continued to be handled until 1978 and clay traffic from the mines south of the station until 1982.

Above - Ivatt 'Class 2' No. 41314 awaiting departure with the 3.39 pm to Bideford.

Tony Molyneaux

Page 72, top - The WR influence at Torrington, that region had taken control of the lines west of Exeter from 1 January 1963, hence the maroon liveried Hawksworth stock. The milk depot is evident.

Page 72, bottom - Busy times at the station. Just arrived is a mixed train having traversed the former North Devon & Cornwall Junction route from Halwill. from Halwill.

Peter Elliott - 2

The North Devon and Cornwall Junction Line

Immediately south of Torrington, the route of the ND&CJR was carried over the valley on a new viaduct: the original wooden structure it replaced hidden by the trees on the left. The train seen departing for Halwill will soon commence climbing to the first stopping place at Watergate Halt. **Bottom and page 74, top -** Most important of the intermediate stations was Hatherleigh although as might be expected from a single coach train it was hardly likely to generate much income. Ivatt 'Class 2' No. 41312 seen with a typical single coach trailing load, although as seen earlier at Torrington, certain trains on this line would also run mixed. **Page 74, bottom -** Watergate Halt, a single Bulleid coach sufficient for the service to Halwill.

Peter Elliott - 2, Roger Thornton - 2

Okehampton

The single road engine shed, turntable and facilities at Okehampton. The shed here having some similarities with that at Ilfracombe. As with all the depots west of Exeter, Okehampton was a sub-shed of Exmouth Junction, and during BR days would have 2-3 locos, for many years a 'T9' and a couple of 'Moguls' out-stationed in this way. In addition visiting engines would be serviced, including those working trains to and from nearby Meldon Quarry. (The chalked description on No. 80038 making reference to something happening on a Friday.)   The John Knottley collection, courtesy of The Swanage Railway Trust - 1

Meldon

Beyond Okehampton was the famed viaduct of the same name and also the stone quarry, the latter still in use today. The line south of Okehampton as far as Bere Alston closed in 1968, although from the Exeter direction, trains continued to serve Okehampton until 1972, an ignominious end to what had once been a main line. Ironically, it was not until 1970 that rail access to the quarry was provided at the Okehampton end of the site, previous to which trains had to run on to the viaduct and set back. Subsequent to 1970, the track on the viaduct became in effect a head shunt.

Opposite top left - Coming in from the direction of Plymouth and Bere Alston is No. 34023 *'Blackmore Vale'*.
Opposite top right and opposite bottom - 'USA' tank, No. DS234, in the concrete engine shed, and outside in the quarry. This engine, formerly No. 30062, arrived in December 1962 to replace a 'G6' 0-6-0 No. DS682. In turn it was replaced by diesel power in 1966.

The John Knottley collection, courtesy of The Swanage Railway Trust - 1, David Smith - 1

Bere Alston for Callington

The stub of the Callington branch from Bere Alston as far as Gunnislake, is the sole surviving former SR branch line west of Exeter still operating a public service. That from Gunnislake to the original terminus Callington closed in November 1966 and nowadays a new station at Gunnislake exists away from the site of the original.

Above - In the days when the branch was fully open, it was almost possible to travel back in time to the quaint terminus at Callington complete with its overall roof. For many years the branch was operated by '02' class 0-4-4T locos but as these were withdrawn so their replacement came in the form of the Ivatt 'Class 2'.

Pages 78 / 79 - The main line junction at Bere Alston with what is no doubt a Callington train waiting in the platform. Conversation was more important than a headcode disc. With the engine not motor-fitted, it was necessary to run-round at either end of the journey.

Peter Elliott - 2

Halwill Junction

Halwill Junction was one of those locations whose railway infrastructure bore no resemblance to the size of the local community. Again a railway crossroads, with lines to and from Okehampton, Bude, Padstow, and Torrington, all of which have now long ceased to exist. **Above** - In happier times, 'N' No. 31840 waits with a Padstow - Okehampton working. **Bottom** - Similar duty for an absolutely filthy No. 34083 *'605 Squadron'*. **Opposite top** - The terminus at Bude, 228 miles from Waterloo, a journey time of between five and eight hours by train. **Opposite bottom** - Believed to be No. 80042 arriving from Halwill with just a single coach. At peak holiday times, ten coaches might be the norm.   The John Knottley collection, courtesy of The Swanage Railway Trust - 2

The Bude Branch and Wadebridge

Above - Taking water at Bude. The goods shed is to the right whilst out of camera on the left was a single road engine shed. **Bottom -** Stabled stock in the 1939 siding added for the exact purpose. **Opposite top -** Travelling back to Halwill and then south west through Launceston we reach Wadebridge where 'Well Tank' No. 30586 is seen outside the goods shed. These diminutive engines were employed here on station shunting duties as well as on there more renowned work with china-clay trains to Bodmin.

Opposite bottom - Breakfast on the footplate perhaps? No. 31844 waits at Wadebridge before setting out on the final part of the journey to Padstow.

The John Knottley collection, courtesy of The Swanage Railway Trust, Peter Elliott, Roger Thornton, Les Elsey

Wadebridge Loco

The locomotive facilities at Wadebridge dated from 1895 and were subsequently extended in the form seen here in 1907. Classified by BR as 72F under Southern Region Exmouth Junction control, the code changed to 84E in September 1963 when the Western Region at Laira took charge. During the 1950s the allocation was of the Beattie 'Well Tank' and 'O2' types, supplemented by visiting engines, mainly 'Moguls' and the 'Pacific' types: to cater for the latter a new 70' turntable was also installed.

As the older engines were withdrawn, so Ivatt 'Class 2' tank engines appeared whilst under the Western Region it was '1361' and '57xx' classes that dominated.

Facilities were limited but included a wheel hoist seen in the view lower left. Coaling was in the main labour intensive the only mechanical assistance being an elevator.

Opposite top - 'Well Tank' No. 30586 in the rain outside the shed, with No. 31842 in the background.

Opposite bottom - 'West Country' No. 34033 *'Chard'* and 'N' No. 38155 stand together at the depot.

This page - Another 'N', No. 31842, but seemingly looking somewhat dejected outside the west end of the shed. Loco access to the facilitates was possible from either end of the site, the turntable being located just behind the photographer.

The John Knottley collection, courtesy of The Swanage Railway Trust - 2, David Smith

Padstow

The literal end of the line at Padstow, and the westernmost outpost of the Southern 260 miles from Waterloo. Here it was possible to arrive or depart in a through carriage all the way to London Waterloo, travelling by the 'Atlantic Coast Express' or indeed other workings. The length of the journey naturally dependent upon the number of stops. As an example, the Summer 1959 timetable showed a departure from Waterloo at 11.00 am (11.05 am on certain days of the week), with arrival at Padstow at 5.07 pm in both cases. It was possible to arrive earlier, but that would mean a 1.10 am departure arriving at 9.22 am. Despite the hour of the latter, there was no sleeping car service.

Opposite top - No. 34033 '*Chard*' in the process of departing the station. Despite the obvious lack of carriage roof boards, plus the number of vehicles involved, both Mk1and Bulleid vehicles, this may well indicate the commencement of a through working to Waterloo.

Opposite bottom - 'N' No. 31843 in the course of running around its train. The signal box is to typical LSWR design, (SRS type '4' style) but built of local stone. Opened in 1889 with a frame of 18 levers, it sent and received trains on the five mile section to the next signal box at Wadebridge West. Padstow signal box closed from 9 January 1966.

Above - The crew of 'N' No. 31843 are clearly amused by the antics of the seagull perched on the tender of their engine as they await the tip to set their train back and then run-around. In the background is the end of the Fish Merchants Offices.

The John Knottley collection, courtesy of The Swanage Railway Trust - 2, Peter Elliott - 1

Padstow
Above - A plethora of barrows and a colourful array of posters plus an attractive station garden.

Bottom - Run round loop and sidings. The rake of coaches is standing on one of the sidings formerly used for fish and perishables traffic. Most of this traffic was lost in consequence of the 1955 railway strike.

Opposite page, top - A 'Mogul' on the 70' vacuum operated turntable, much of the station site being on reclaimed land.

Opposite page, bottom - 'N' No. 31843 awaiting departure for Wadebridge and beyond.

Peter Elliott - 4

T9s at Padstow

The overnight train from Waterloo has already been referred to briefly and for many years a similar method was employed for sending newspapers to North Cornwall. Instead of arriving direct however, in the 1930s the newspapers would leave London at 1.30 am, transfer on to the 6.02 am freight at Okehampton and thence the 7.45 am passenger train to Launceston, finally arriving at Padstow at 9.01 am.

On page 91 is a member of the 'T9' class, a type long associated with West Country lines although No. 30729 only arrived to spend the last months of its working life in the area.

Recorded sometime between April 1960 and April 1961 for No. 30729 the working was not reported. In the background to the view opposite bottom are the various buildings belonged to Messrs Pawlyn Bros, used as a fish curing depot and stores.

Goods traffic from Padstow ceased in 1964 after which the various through workings were run down ceasing completely in September 1966. From 1 October 1966 the only rail access to Padstow was now via Bodmin, the route from Halwill to Wadebridge having closed completely. It was inevitable that Padstow would not survive much longer and complete closure occurred on 20 January 1967.

Roger Thornton - 2

Bottom - The route across the broad creek to Little Petheridge and eventually Wadebridge. Much of the track formation survives today as part of the Camel trail for walkers and cyclists.

Peter Elliott

Page 92 overleaf - No. 34033 *'Chard'* leaving. It was to be hoped that the passenger compliment would increase later compared with that seen in the first coach at this stage of the journey.

The John Knottley collection, courtesy of The Swanage Railway Trust - 2

Boscarne Junction

Boscarne Junction was the location where the connection was made between the LSWR and GWR routes south of Wadebridge, as well as for the mineral line to Wenford Bridge. In the scene above, No. 30587 has taken the northern branch in the direction of Bodmin North and Wenford Bridge. The GWR route from Bodmin General arriving from the left just beyond the signal and ground frame.

Bottom - Boscarne Junction - the signal box which controlled the junction between the two companies lines is in the background, as a shining 'Well Tank', No. 30587 waits with some dedicated china-clay wagons.

Roger Thornton

The Wenford Bridge Branch

Historically, the Wenford Bridge branch was one of the earliest railways in Cornwall, opened between Bodmin and Wadebridge in May 1832 and the section to Wenford Bridge in September of the same year. Controlled by the LSWR from 1847 and formerly absorbed into the LSWR in 1886, it was not until 1895 that there was a physical link between the B & W and LSWR system proper commensurate with the opening of the line to Bude in 1895. China Clay and sand was the principal traffic on the Wenford Bridge branch, a line which was in effect a mineral line throughout its existence.

Above - To operate services on what was a lightly built line only able to accommodate locomotives having a limited axle load, three Beattie design 'Well-Tanks', of 1874 vintage were retained long after their sister engines had been consigned to scrap. This engine, No. 30587 survives today in preservation.

Left - Taking water in Pencarrow Woods, the water coming from the nearby River Camel. Notice the 3-link couplings that are fitted.

Roger Thornton

Bodmin North

This page and overleaf - The LSWR terminus at Bodmin North was located closed to the town centre than the GWR Bodmin General station, although the luxury of two stations was hardly ever warranted by the town. Apart from a few years when steam railmotors were used, services to Bodmin North were steam operated almost until the very end. Both tank and tender engines were used, the latter usually 'Mogul' types. One exception was in 1946, when 'West Country' No. 21C16 'Bodmin' was named at the station, the only time an engine of the type visited the location. **This page** - Ivatt 'Class 2', No. 41275 on a Wadebridge service, these engines had replaced the 'O2' class on the branch. **Overleaf** - Another member of the class, No. 41275 runs round it strain whilst a 'Mogul', complete with storm sheet, waits in the yard.   Peter Elliott - 4